Dedication

To my fellow lightworkers

Table Of Contents

„You can't cross the sea merely by standing and staring at the water."

R. Tagore

Introduction: Beginning of Our Journey

Peace is not something that can be 'achieved' but rather something that one must BECOME

The human mind is an awesome thing. It is the wellspring of creativity and ingenuity. It brings forth magnificent creations of all kinds. Everything we see in the man-made world is a reflection of the mind. Without human imagination, the world as we know it would not exist. This is the obvious truth, but then what can be said about all the suffering in the world? If the manifestation of things, events, and circumstances depends primarily on the mind, then war, crime, and the like must also be correlated with prevailing 'states of mind'. If beauty and destruction both stem from the mind, then it is of utmost importance that we monitor our thoughts, for they are the seeds that will inevitably bear the fruits of our future circumstances.

It can be said that any one person's overall character and demeanor is but a reflection of the total of his or her thoughts. Outward expression through action is the natural consequence of one's innermost thoughts, whether consciously known or not, and this work tends to perpetuate the feelings that initiated it. No amount of action or thinking can bring complete peace of mind although certain thoughts can aid in its discovery. It's the topic we will be discussing in this chapter

Remember what I said about action being the natural consequence of our innermost thoughts? Itis important to keep in mind as we go along, because, for us to allow spontaneous and effortless expression, we must first address the underlying thoughts that are the causes of our forced, stress-inducing actions. We MUST shift our thinking to those of nature that more closely resembles the truth of what we are; and then we will begin to become like the planets, moons, stars, and galaxies that flow through space without a worry in the world. We will start to realize who we are. Only greater happiness and peace of mind can result from this realization.

Chapter 1:

Your Perception

Take full responsibility for your life is the catalyst for rapid mental, emotional, and spiritual growth.

Perception is your reality. Your overall perception is a consequence of how you think and interprets the world around you. We call people with a negative perception of the world pessimists, and those with a more liberal view we call optimists. What is the difference between these two different types of people?

Many people go through their entire lives unconsciously choosing to give away their power. They don't even realize that they have the authority to choose their thoughts and feelings and thus create their reality. The reality is a subjective experience. Each of us sees the world in a different way, and that perception is what determines our inner experience. Circumstances in and of themselves do not have any power. It's our interpretation of these conditions that determines whether or not we will be empowered or disempowered by them.

Dear reader, YOU have the strength and always will. How you see the world, in fact, creates the world you see. Your beliefs determine who you're going to become and what actions you are going to take. What you see in your reality at this time is nothing more than the consequence of all your past thoughts and emotions. What you have created thus far does not make you happy, it's because you have chosen disempowering beliefs and negative emotions and have thus created an environment that is unsupportive and frustrating to be in. That environment may be a physical one or an internal one, but that is irrelevant. Remember that it is not the circumstances themselves that have the power. How you see circumstances is simply a reflection of what has been going on inside your mind. Even in the worst of times, you can find the beauty. Life is not one way or the other; life is simply seen a certain way as a result of your interpretation of it.

I hope you can handle the truth. The fact is that YOU are a MIRACLE. All of us have unlimited strength aka potential. I'm speaking of something much more significant than the collection of thoughts and emotions that make up your personality. I'm talking about your 'Higher Self,' which is what you'll be learning to get in touch with throughout this book. Accessing this part of yourself is the necessary prerequisite for lasting happiness and peace of mind, but to do that, you'll need to acquire some new perspectives.

Our ego tends to cherish particular beliefs, whether they are accurate or not. It's bad news for most of us. It means we are quite literally living an illusion. We walk around thinking false thoughts, and we pay the price.

The thoughts we think to form the emotions we feel, and vice versa, which in turn manifest as physical action. Whether you know it or not, your life is a direct reflection of the content of your thoughts and innermost feelings. You may believe, as many do, that it is the circumstances of your life that bring you happiness or a lack of it. You may look at your life and think, "why in the world should I feel happy when all these `bad' things are happening to me?"

It's probably tough for you to believe that you are creating your reality with your thoughts and emotions, although, I encourage you to let go of your cherished beliefs for a moment, for they may significantly hinder your spiritual evolution and thus your chances for lasting happiness. I'm not asking you to believe anything. I'm only asking you to consider this new perspective. Could it be that you have been playing tricks on yourself, causing yourself to believe in a limited version of yourself?

The sheer miracle of your existence is proof that you are indeed blessed. The human mind is very limited in that it can only ponder its current perception of reality and cannot stretch very far beyond what it 'thinks' it knows. To do so requires intense humility and self-honesty. The mind is a closed system with many inherent flaws and should therefore not be so readily clung to. Your thoughts are just mental constructs you have adopted throughout your life from other people and your environment. It does not at all prove the truth of your thoughts. In fact, it reveals the likelihood of your thoughts being very far from the actual nature of reality.

You have no idea how powerful you are.

Chapter 2:

Let Go Of Your Limiting Beliefs

"Live your beliefs and you can turn the world around."

Henry David Thoreau

Before we can let go of our limiting beliefs and start thriving like we were meant to, we need to gain an understanding of how emotions work and what the relationship is between emotion and thought. In this way, we can avoid wasting time with tedious methods and techniques and create positive changes within ourselves rapidly.

For many years, I fell into the trap of believing that I had to work with my thoughts directly and actively change them to be happy. While this strategy did work to some degree, it was a slow and painful process. If I had known back then what I know now, I would have taken a more direct route to peace of mind route that leads deep into the core of our problems as human beings.

The real problem we face as human beings in this earthly existence is our storehouse of negative emotions. Our feelings come from the thoughts running through our head. However, the opposite is true as well. The emotions we feel trigger endless streams of thoughts, which thus reinforce the initial feeling. It is easy to see then how we can become trapped in a vicious cycle. The problem with trying to reverse this cycle by working with the thoughts directly is that our thoughts are often not accurate representations of what is going on in the first place. Thoughts are often nothing more than rationalizations based on false perceptions. What is real are the emotions we feel in any given situation. We tend to attempt to justify these feelings with the stories we tell ourselves, however, the stories we tell ourselves aren't the reality.

We feel the way we feel for very good reasons, although these reasons are often not consciously known. The good news is that we don't need to know why we feel the way we do; we only need to acknowledge the way we feel and decide whether or not this particular feeling is something we wish to hold onto or something we would rather let go of. Could positive change be this simple?

While it is certainly important to practice seeing the world in a more positive light by changing the way we think about things, this is sometimes a futile effort due to the massive amounts of emotional resistance buried in our unconscious minds. These resistances are just negative emotions we carry around with us that alter our perception of things without our awareness. The truth just cannot shine forth when it is hidden by dark clouds of negativity. Resistance in the form of negative emotions is like the chain that binds us to our one room cell with no windows. No matter how badly we desire better days, the sun won't shine in such a place until we let go of our current perceptions and emotionalized positions and choose to be open to your inner self; you'll be okay.

Chapter 3:

Love is The Solution

"Love isn't something you find. Love is something that finds you."

Loretta Young

Many of us have been fooling ourselves for a long time by thinking that love is something we need to gain from someone else (and not from ourselves). Nothing could be further from the Truth. Someone can love us deeply and yet we can remain in depression if we do not see ourselves as worthy of that love. It is the person who loves that is the receiver of love. The person who is loved still does not experience love until they choose to reciprocate that energy. It is by giving that we receive.

You have probably noticed that the most of the people are constantly on the lookout for their next potential lover. People are always seeking for love, but the fact that someone is seeking for it guarantees they will not find it. Love is not something you can acquire. Love is something you become, and you do that by giving love to others. By giving love, you increase your ability to do so. By practicing something as simple as thinking kind thoughts about others, you generate greater love within yourself. When you realize that love is something within you that is increased by consistent use, then you will stop all your useless seeking and become a giver, which is the simple key to unleashing your full potential and receiving all that you desire, including peace of mind.

Giving love to all creatures is a conscious choice that I have made, and I am made more whole and happy each day I stay right to this decision. I suggest that you make the decision to do the same. You might just start by thinking one kind thought about someone you care for. Then expand that and mentally send love to everyone you know. Then send it to all the animals of the world. Then begin participating in small acts of kindness. Give cash to a homeless man. Volunteer. Buy your significant other a gift just because you can. Strive for unconditional love. Give as much as you are able and your mind will quickly be put at ease.

The secret to harmonious and peaceful living is giving to the others.

Chapter 4:

Beauty is Everywhere

"Beauty is in the strangest places. A piece of garbage floating in the wind. It exists everywhere. You have to develop an eye for it and be able to see it."

Alan Ball

How you perceive the world is your choice. It's very easy to go through life reacting to our environment and believing that the external conditions are somehow causing us to feel a certain way. But we will only gain control over our emotional states when we understand that the world is not actually how we perceive it to be. No one's perception is the 'correct' perception because perception is merely an interpretation.

What we look for is what we find. If we look for things to be upset about, we will surely find them. There is no limit to the mind's ability to come up with ideas that make you upset in some way. There is also no limit to the mind's ability to come up with things to be grateful for. The mind is like an online search engine. Whatever you tell it to look for is what it will bring to your attention. If you type into your organic search engine, "what can I be grateful for today?" you have no choice but to get an answer to the question. Beauty springs forth when you actively seek it out.

It's well-known by everyone that hindsight often reveals the hidden beauty in seemingly 'negative' events. A bad breakup once left me in a deep depression for over a year. I couldn't see the beauty in that at the time, but now it is so clear to me. That single event spurred me on to take full responsibility for my life and consciously create my future. I would not even be writing this if it were not for that dark period in my life. Sometimes it is in our darkest days that we find the light. If I would not have been so caught up in my negative perceptions at the time, then

perhaps I would have chosen to see it all as a blessing in disguise. It is not easy to remain positive in the face of great adversity, but when you realize that it is simply a matter of choice, it becomes possible.

Don't wait for some unfortunate event to wake you up! Many people wait until life knocks them down before they ever decide to take a good look at how they've been living. Choose to see the beauty in all things, starting now! It is the only way to be truly happy. But what a blessing it is to know that happiness is only a decision away!

Look for the hidden lessons in all situations. Always choose to see the positive side of things. Don't take your life for granted. When you wake up each morning, take a minute to thank you for your life, no matter how bad things may seem. When you get in the car to drive to work, give thanks for your reliable transportation and steady income, no matter how badly you wish you were still in bed. When you see the scenery outside of your window, give thanks for the beauty. When you eat your dinner, appreciate the texture, smell, and taste. Tell your family you love them. Joy lies in the simple things. You are blessed to be here. Know that. Internalize ft. Make gratitude a habitual attitude and you will know happiness.

Life itself is a tremendous learning opportunity. It is extremely helpful to begin looking at 'bad' events as nothing more than a chance to learn something and evolve as a spiritual being. 'Bad' and other negative descriptions are of course just interpretations that can be altered by conscious choice. Eliminate any negative words from your vocabulary and replace them with phrases like opportunity for growth, challenge to

Chapter 5:

Can You Achieve Greatness with Peace of Mind?

"Some are born great, some achieve greatness, and some have greatness thrust upon them."

William Shakespeare

Let's say you have a goal to earn a degree of money in your business this year. Is it possible to be effective if you're not constantly thinking one step ahead and planning for the future? Actually, yes it is, and it's deceivingly simple.

Set your short and long-term goals and write them out on a piece of paper. It's important because if you do not write them down, they will be bouncing around in your head all day long! Putting them onto paper clears your mind and automatically decreases your overall levels of stress. Now, work backward from those goals and come up with a weekly plan, breaking that down into a maximum of 5 daily tasks for each day of the week Write this plan out on paper. Now you have done almost all the thinking you need to do! Simply begin with task #1 and work through your list until all tasks are completed. What more is there to do? It may require an hour of planning each week, but that leaves you with 167 hours each week to simply let life unfold naturally! No stress required.

Thinking won't get you to your goals, but it will certainly make the process a lot more stressful than it needs to be. ACTION is all that is necessary, and that is not in conflict with spiritual principles. Surpassing the chatter in your head does not mean that you are giving up control of your life. In fact, it means you are finally exercising maximum control! You can now LIVE instead of just thinking about living. Life is lived at this very moment.

Stop comparing yourself now to where you used to be or to where you think you should be. Neither of those people are actually you, and so neither of those thoughts can bring you any peace of mind. If you truly desire some sort of change in your lifestyle or circumstances, then accept where you are right now and simply choose to move in a new direction. Change is actually continuous. It doesn't happen in leaps and spurts as we imagine it to. It's not like we need to make all these drastic changes to reach some far off destination. The sailor who is off course doesn't need to panic. He simply adjusts the direction of his ship and allows the natural forces of wind and water to carry him to his desired destination. Your intention to change is sufficient to create that change. Strenuous effort is not necessary.

Chapter 6:

Mastering Your Physical Body

Inner peace cannot be achieved with without healthy body.

The real you wants to express itself through your physical body. The way you treat and care for your body is an expression of your inner state. When you are healthy, you can enjoy a higher vibration than if you let your physical state deteriorate. Your body is the physical vehicle that temporarily carries your soul. When you are healthy and your energy vibrates at a high frequency you have optimal conditions that allow your Higher Self to shine through. You cannot progress to your potential without much thought being given to your physical body. That means giving effort towards looking after your health. Health is essential to the quality of your life. Many people, especially as they age, find that their body deteriorates rapidly. It means that you have to endure less mobility and a reduction in energy. It's not very difficult for you to achieve health. If you don't have it today, you won't, however, have it by tomorrow. It requires a continued effort, and it will be achieved soon.

Health is made in three ways:

1. Your diet.

2. Movement.

3. Your lifestyle.

Your body is important because it is the vehicle that carries you through your life. It is also the vehicle that allows you to be you.

Nutrition is import for the optimal functioning of your body. Optimal functioning means being the best you can be. You do not need to compare yourself with anyone else.

Your body consists of cells. A cell is the basic building block of your body. Your cells are continually regenerating. It is estimated that every three months the cells in your body are completely replaced. In other words, you get a whole new body. Your cells process nutrients. They absorb what they need, and they eliminate waste.

Nutrition is important because the nutrients that you take in are responsible for the maintenance of your physical vehicle. Without your body performing correctly you will significantly lower the quality of your life, or you will shorten your life. Often both. Without your body working properly you can't get what you need and certainly can't get what you want. We are going to cover the basics of nutrition so that you know what to do.

To live you need to take in six things:

1. Oxygen.

2. Water.

3. Vitamins and minerals.

4. Carbohydrates.

5. Fat.

6. Protein.

To stress the importance of these six things, look at it this way. **Life lasts about:**

1. Three minutes without oxygen.

2. Three days without water.

3. Thirty days without food.

You are concerned with more than just life. You are concerned with getting the most from your life and living a quality life. For that to occur you need to educate yourself on what's essential so that you can maximize your opportunity for living.

Chapter 7:

The Air You Breathe

"Breathe into your balls!"

Elliot Hulse

You need oxygen to live; that's pretty straightforward. For optimum performance, you need an adequate oxygen supply. Without enough oxygen, your thought process is inhibited. That's proven in tests with scuba divers and astronauts. Proving for yourself is easy. Just go for a jog and finish with an uphill run until you are out of breath. Try to do a simple mathematical calculation. It will be much more challenging than usual because you are temporarily deprived of oxygen.

To maximize your oxygen intake, you need to breathe properly. That means changing your breathing from shallow to deep. Deep breathing allows you to get more oxygen by filling your lungs to capacity. It's conducive to transferring more oxygen to your blood and, therefore, the cells in your body. When you are physically fit, you have the increased ability to utilize oxygen. You might notice that healthy people are often vibrant. The correct way to breathe is in through your nose and out of your mouth. Your nose has a filter system that clears the air you breathe. It is also responsible for heating and moisturizing the air before it travels to your lungs.

You probably breathe using only your chest. It's the incorrect way to breathe.

You need to breathe with your diaphragm. You can tell if you are doing this correctly because your stomach fills and empties; you can see it. Your chest stays as it is.

Breathing slowly and deeply using your diaphragm is an excellent way to calm yourself and alleviate stress. If you watch yourself in a stressful situation, you will find that you are shallow breathing.

Breathing Techniques

Try the two different types of breathing now.

Put your hand on your chest and breath in so that you can feel your chest expanding. Breathe in and out; feel your chest moving. It's shallow breathing.

Breathe in through your nose and out through your mouth. Put one hand on your stomach and the other hand on your chest.

Breathe in so that you can feel your stomach area fill with air. It's sometimes easier to feel when you are lying down. Make sure that your chest does not move when you do this.

Chapter 8:

Hydration

„Unfortunately, I think there's not enough education about hydration. When I was young, we knew nothing about it. We all know that there's cases of athletes having serious issues because of dehydration and even dying."

Landon Donovan

If I had to nominate the easiest and quickest way for you to feel great, I would say drink more water. It would have to be the most neglected yet useful self-improvement technique in the world.

Seventy percent of your body is water. To function optimally you need to be hydrated; that is, have enough water. Your body uses water to maintain balance in its systems. It transports essential nutrients throughout your body and rids it of waste and toxins. It acts as a lubricant for your body, moistening eyes, mouth, nose, and skin. It helps maintain adequate blood volume. It helps you regulate your temperature, especially in warm weather. It contributes to preventing constipation.

Drinking lots of water will help you avoid extra fat deposits. Your kidneys function at their best when you are hydrated. One thing they do is metabolize stored fat into energy. When your kidneys don't function properly, your liver helps it along, but it can't metabolize fat. That means you will have a higher propensity to store fat. When you don't have enough water, you are dehydrated. It makes you tired, and you feel sluggish. When you are dehydrated, you cannot think properly, and you lose the ability to concentrate. You need only suffer a two or three percent loss of water from your body for your performance to suffer. You're "wasting" water all the time. It's done through sweat, breathing and when you go to the toilet. You lose about half a liter from breathing everyday. Many people have trouble discerning thirst from hunger. They eat instead of drink. When you get thirsty, this is your body's survival mechanism ensuring that you get more water. The thirst mechanism provides you survive; it doesn't ensure you are hydrated for maximum efficiency. In other words, by the time you are thirsty you have been dehydrated for some time.

You can get water in food, especially food like fruit and vegetables. However, this will not ensure you have an adequate supply of water.
You need to drink at least eight glasses of water per day; more if you are a big, heavy person. Tea, coffee, and soft drink do not count towards your water consumption.

Create an excellent habit and start the day with two glasses of water before you do anything else in the morning. It is what I do, and it means that you get a great start to your day.

Here are seven more facts you need to know about water:

1. Seventy-five percent of Americans are chronically dehydrated. This most likely applies to half the world's population.

2. In thirty-seven percent of Americans, the thirst mechanism is so weak that people often mistake it for hunger.

3. Even mild dehydration will slow down your metabolism as much as three percent.

4. One glass of water will shut down midnight hunger pangs for almost one hundred percent of the dieters studied in a University of Washington study.

5. Lack of water is the number one trigger of daytime fatigue.

6. Preliminary research indicates that eight to ten glasses of water a day could significantly ease back and joint pain for up to eighty percent of sufferers.

7. A mere two percent drop in body water can trigger fuzzy short-term memory, trouble with basic math and difficulty focusing on the computer screen or a printed page.

You need to act to make positive change. You need to build a habit. Being awake and in awareness, you can effect change in your life. Drink more water. Try this yourself and see if it works.

Chapter 9:

Various Minerals And Vitamins

Vitamins and minerals are vital for you to function properly.

Fat-soluble vitamins are stored for varying amounts of time in the fat tissue of your body and your liver. When your body needs them, they can be called upon. Vitamin A, D, E, and K are fat-soluble vitamins.

Vitamin A is sometimes called retinol. It is necessary for healthy skin, hair, bones and teeth. It plays a significant part in your eyesight. It is found in milk, egg yolks, liver and other organ meats. You can get plenty of it in guava, apricots, nectarines and cantaloupe. You can also find it in vegetables like carrots, spinach, and pumpkins.

Vitamin D is responsible for healthy bones and teeth. It enables you to absorb calcium and is essential for the proper use of vitamin A. It is found in liver, egg yolks, tuna, salmon and fortified milk. Although it's not food, you can get vitamin D from the sun.

Vitamin E protects the tissues in your body as your eyes, skin and liver. It is also responsible for protecting your lungs from pollutants. It enables you to store vitamin A, and you can find it in vegetable oils and dark, leafy green vegetables like spinach and nuts.

Vitamin K is what allows your blood to clot. You will find it is plentiful in dark green vegetables like broccoli and spinach. It's also found in lettuce and cabbage. If you like cheese you have found another source of vitamin K. Water-soluble vitamins are not stored in your body. They travel through your blood stream and don't stay in your body as long. The excess is lost when you urinate. That means you need to replenish them much more often. Vitamin C and the vitamin B group are the water-soluble vitamins. Vitamin C helps your body fight infection, and it helps your body resist infection. It strengthens bones and muscles. It aids in healing, and it helps with the elasticity of your skin. You find it in sweet fruits like oranges, tangerines, lemons, grapefruit, honeydew melon, watermelon, tomatoes, strawberries, and raspberries. Vegetable like broccoli and green peppers are loaded with vitamin C, and of course so are fruit juices.

The vitamin B group comprises of vitamin B1, vitamin B2, niacin, vitamin B6, folic acid, vitamin B12, biotin and pantothenic acid. The B group vitamins are responsible for your metabolic activity. That means they allow you to make and use energy as it is required. They also help with a variety of other functions like digestion. You find the B vitamins in fish, especially tuna, and meat like beef and chicken. Whole-wheat grains and dark green leafy vegetables are excellent sources for the B group of vitamins.

Calcium helps relieve insomnia and nervous tension. It allows you to form healthy bones and teeth and is found in low-fat dairy products and oily fish with bones like sardines and salmon. Of course you can't go wrong if you eat dark green leafy vegetables – they are also a source of calcium.

Phosphorous helps your body repair itself, and you find it in fish, poultry, whole grains, eggs, nuts and seeds.

Magnesium is essential in the metabolism of vitamin C and some minerals. It promotes a healthy cardiovascular system. It helps you with the relief of stress and depression. It also maintains healthy teeth and prevents kidney stones. You can find it in nuts and seeds, bran and whole grains. Dark green vegetables and lemons are an excellent source of it.

Sodium allows your muscles to function, and you find it in ordinary table salt. It's also in shellfish, carrots, and celery.

Potassium enables you to relax and contract your muscles. It aids you in the maintenance of fluid and nutrient levels within your cells. It's found in abundance in bananas, apricots, oranges and potatoes.

Trace minerals include iron, manganese, copper, zinc and selenium. As their name suggests you only need slight amounts of theses minerals.

Iron promotes resistance to disease. It prevents fatigue, and it helps produce hemoglobin, which is the part of your red blood cells that carries oxygen from your lungs to the rest of your body. You find iron in red meat, dried beans, egg yolks, asparagus, whole-grain bread, apricots, raisins, oysters, and spinach.

Manganese aids your muscle reflexes and prevents fatigue. You will get plenty of it eating leafy vegetables, beetroot, and nuts. You also find it in egg yolks.

Copper promotes the absorption of iron and, therefore, helps you keep your energy levels up. You find copper in seafood, prunes, liver and whole wheat.

Zinc is essential for optimum sexual function in men over thirty-five years of age. Found in oysters and other seafood, lean meats, yeast, pumpkin seeds and whole grains.

Selenium helps your body tissue retain its elasticity. It is found in onions, tomatoes, whole-grain cereals, garlic, meat, and poultry.

It's not by any means even close to a comprehensive list. If you want a detailed explanation, then you can look in a specialist publication. The point here is simple. You need vitamins and minerals. You find them in the food you eat. The common theme is variety, comprising fruits, vegetables and meats, including seafood.

You find the least quantity of vitamins and minerals in processed foods like white bread and cakes.

Some vitamins and minerals are lost when you cook foods, and more are lost when you overcook food. Older produce has less nutritional value than fresh produce. Your requirement for vitamins and minerals increases if you exercise or you are stressed.

Watch what you think as you make a choice of what to eat. You can change your eating habits from processed food to that of food that is rich in nutrients.

Chapter 10:

Nutrition – Lifeforce

You are what you eat.

You use up energy all the time, even when you are seated, doing nothing or sleeping. It's called your metabolism. It is the rate that you turn food energy into usable energy in your body. Food energy is measured in a unit called calories. A sixty-five kilogram person uses about sixty calories an hour just sleeping, or five hundred calories for an hour of jogging. Of course, these estimates vary significantly for individuals. It's a guide only. If you are big, you use more energy. If you have a larger amount of muscle you use more energy just to stay alive, it's a proven fact.

One kilogram of body fat is 7700 calories. That means you have a lot of sleeping to do if you wish to shed that excess weight. That's a joke. As you can see, there is a lot of activity in your excess weight. To lose weight you need to use more energy than you consume.

Generally speaking, the more oxygen that is present and available the more you will use fat as energy. The less oxygen present, the more you will use carbohydrates. So when you are sitting doing nothing, you will have plenty of oxygen available and will burn fat. Going for a jog, which requires more work, will mean that your oxygen demand will increase, and, therefore, you will have less available, and you will use more carbohydrates as energy. Don't get confused with the total amount of energy that you use. If you do more work, and jogging is more work than walking, then you will burn more calories overall. If you live a sedentary lifestyle, you don't need much energy.

Carbohydrates

Carbohydrates provide you with energy. You can find carbohydrates in fruit, vegetables, rice, potatoes, and pasta. All carbohydrates provide four calories per gram of carbohydrate. To put that into real terms means that to get twenty grams of carbohydrate, which is eighty calories, you could eat any of the following:

One slice of bread.

One apple.

½ a cup of cooked rice.

20 cups of alfalfa.

Five sticks of celery

Two whole cucumbers.

Four lettuces.

Four tomatoes.

You need about four hundred grams of carbohydrates per day if you are active, and only one hundred and fifty to two hundred grams of carbohydrates if you are inactive.

Carbohydrates like bread, pasta and rice provide you with lots of energy and not many nutrients. Fruit and vegetables provide you with many nutrients but not as much energy.

If you are inactive, like someone who works in an office, you don't need many carbohydrates. If you get all of your energy from bread and pasta, then you are missing out on the nutrients found in other food sources. If your carbohydrate requirement is two hundred grams per day, then the following will suffice. Please note I am not recommending you eat this, just pointing out what constitutes two hundred grams of carbohydrate.

Two pieces of toast for breakfast, with a glass of orange juice.

The bread from your sandwich at lunchtime.

Two cups of cooked rice at dinnertime.

As you can see this does not leave you much room for the multitude of nutrients that can be found in fruit and vegetables. Bread and rice are energy rich. If you are inactive, you need to concentrate on using predominately fruits and vegetables for your energy source so that you get enough nutrients.

Some carbohydrates turn to energy very quickly in your body. There is a scale to measure this called the glycemic index. Foods that have a high value on this index are rapidly turned to energy and foods that have a low-value last longer as energy sources in your body. The index is a percentage comparison against pure glucose, which has the index value of one hundred.

When you have a large amount of energy quickly entering your blood stream, you have too much energy for your body to use at once. To stabilize your energy levels, the hormone insulin is released. The presence of insulin promotes the storage of your excess energy as fat. When you have a large amount of energy, enter your bloodstream quickly you also have a noticeable lift in your mood and energy. Like a roller coaster, if you have a sharp and sudden climb you will also have a vast and sudden fall. The insulin released ensures this. The massive influx of energy over-stimulates the production of insulin and, therefore, you have a hard fall that results in you feeling tired and lethargic, often unable to think correctly. Your roller coaster ride now continues as you subconsciously seek relief from your low by eating high glycemic index foods.

You can lower the glycemic index of food if you ingest it with fat and protein. Some studies have shown that eating a low glycemic index diet helps towards feeling full and keeping the synthesis of cholesterol down. If you have stable energy levels without wild fluctuations you will derive greater enjoyment from your day. You will have more energy to do the things you want. You often have an afternoon slump. It happens, usually at work, around two o'clock to four o'clock in the evening. Sometimes you attribute this to boredom, lack of sleep or who knows what. It usually means that you have had a high carbohydrate lunch comprising of high glycemic index foods and little protein or fat, and you are now suffering a low on your roller coaster ride. Change the source of your carbohydrates and add some protein and a little fat to the meal. It will aid in slowing the energy release and give you a more even spread of energy throughout the day. You will avoid the afternoon slump.

Chapter 11:

Healthy Fats for Peaceful mind

You need fat in your diet to live. Your brain is ninety percent fat, and your body needs it for energy. Fat is high in energy because every gram of fat has nine calories. By weight, fat has more than double the energy than carbohydrate, so you need to eat fat in moderation. A hamburger typically contains three hundred calories from fat alone. (Every one of them tastes great.)

Fat is important to many of your body's systems. It is responsible for healthy skin and hair and is essential for cell membrane reproduction.

There are two types of fat, and you need both of them:

1. Saturated fat.

Saturated fat comes from animal sources like meat. If you consume too much saturated fat, it can be a contributor to raised cholesterol levels. Saturated fat needs to be consumed in moderation.

2. Unsaturated fat.

Unsaturated fat comes from fish and vegetables like avocado, nuts and sunflower seeds. Unsaturated fat can be a factor in lowering your cholesterol levels.

An average inactive person needs about fifty grams of fat per day.

Hamburger has about thirty-six grams of fat.

A tablespoon of peanut butter has about seven grams of fat.

]One teaspoon of butter or margarine has four grams of fat.

One cup of milk has about seven grams of fat.

An avocado has thirty grams of fat.

A plain donut has six grams of fat.

A slice of pizza has twelve grams of fat.

As you can see it doesn't take much for the fat to add up. Don't forget about your protein intake!

Chapter 12:

Getting rid of Toxins

You need to minimize toxins. Some reduction is better than no decrease in the toxins you consume.

Alcohol is not only a poison to your body it contains seven calories per milliliter. The calories you consume from alcohol have no nutritional value at all. You need to exercise moderation when you drink alcohol. Under the influence of alcohol, your Higher Self is not able to guide you at all. During social occasions, an easy way to control your drinking in a positive way is to make a rule that you will consume a glass of water before your first drink and a glass of water before every other drink you have. This does three things:

1. It physically fills you up.

2. It slows the rate at which you drink.

3. It keeps you hydrated and helps flush your system.

Tobacco is a toxin that has been shown to adversely affect you. You need to stop it now – cut it out completely. You are poisoning your body if you smoke cigarettes. When you know, you are poisoning your body, and you still do it then you need to work on your self-esteem. Deliberately destroying your physical vehicle means that you subconsciously don't like yourself.

Social drugs. Don't take them. Your Higher Self can't be present when you are under the influence of a drug that changes your reality. Ask yourself what is so wrong that you need to escape from this world. Then start reading this book again and put the techniques into practice.

Processed foods and additives. Minimize them. Look at your overall food intake and make a definite attempt to get most of your food from natural sources. Processed foods often have loads of energy and not much nutrition. Additives are an addition to many foods and are tough to avoid. Make an attempt to know what they do and to avoid them where possible. A good place to start is MSG, which is coded 621 here in Australia. Many people react strongly to MSG, complaining of all sorts of difficulties like sluggishness, asthma and skin rashes. Read the labels of the food you eat and you will discover much about what goes into your body.

Reading the labels of the food you buy requires you to slow your shopping trip and focus on what you buy. You decide if you want to read the labels or not. Once you have done this several times, you will know which items are preferable. Often very simple things have an enormous difference in additives from one brand to the next. Reading the labels is your only option.

Caffeine. Give it up or drink only one or two cups of real coffee per day. Instant coffee dissolves in your cup, and then you drink the whole lot. When real coffee is created, hot water is pushed through coffee, and the coffee is discarded – the water is flavored. Now you make your choice. By giving up instant coffee and only drinking coffee when you are out, you drastically reduce the amount of coffee you drink without giving it away.

🄐

Chapter 13:

So What to Do Now?

There are two things you need to consider. You need to be the right weight, and you need to be healthy. The two are often connected. Generally, when you are over or underweight, you are not healthy. Many millions of hours of information abound on the virtues of why you should be at your correct weight, so I don't need to go into the health pitfalls of being overweight.

When you are at your optimal weight, you still need to keep your body healthy. You do this by monitoring what you ingest.

You need to have a look at what you eat. Buy a calorie counter from your local bookstore – they are inexpensive. This type of book will give you a guide to what's in your food and how many calories you need.

The number of calories that you take in and the number that you burn up determine your weight. If you burn more than you take in, then you lose weight. If you take in too many, you gain weight.

Aim at getting fifty percent of your calories from carbohydrates, thirty percent of your calories from fat and twenty percent of your calories from protein. You may have to make adjustments to this. If you need more energy, you will need to consume more calories from carbohydrates. If you do many different exercises, you will require more protein and perhaps also more carbohydrates.

If you seek weight reduction, then do the following unless you are extremely overweight. Rather than standing on scales look in the mirror and grab your excess fat. It will quickly show you how much you can lose. Scales are deceptive. Muscle weighs more than fat. You are a skeleton with muscle around the bone and a layer of fat around the muscle. You need something to make your shape. It can be either muscle or fat. It's your choice. If you want it to be muscle you need to eat nutritious food and exercise. If you diet severely, do not exercise and forgo eating enough protein you will lose your muscle mass. The more muscle you have, the more calories, you burn without moving, just by being alive. If you let your muscles deteriorate then, your metabolism slows, and you will find that you use less energy for everything you do which makes it easier to store fat.

If you don't already have a healthy diet, this is what you can do to change:

1. Education. You need to start to read information on the subject so that you can know more. When you find, out more you can make better decisions.

2. Don't try to change from unhealthy to healthy in one go. Make small changes to the things that you find easiest first. Do this before you attempt any radical change. Many small changes eventually make your large radical change. Here are some examples:

• I always have two glasses of water first thing in the morning before I do anything. It's easy, and you get a great head start to your daily quota, which is eight glasses per day.

• I have a rule that I have to eat something natural and healthy with every meal. It's easy to order a salad when you go out, and it is easy to steam a pile of vegetables when you are home. If you are thinking "but I hate vegetables," I'll be blunt – if you want to live, and you want some quality from your life, then get with the program and find a way to like them. Covering them with chocolate sauce is better than not eating them.

• Cut down your alcohol and coffee intake; try the method I suggested with the alternating glasses of water.

• If you eat a lot, and you are overweight, try to reduce the portions you have before you change what you eat. It's one step at a time.

• Eat fruit as a snack., you don't need sugar.
• Eat some protein with every meal.
• Substitute vegetables where you eat rice, pasta and bread.
• Eat the majority of your calories before dinnertime. Have a light dinner only. It will help you lose weight and sleep better. The way to do this is to look at your total daily intake and subtract from dinner and add this quantity in part to lunch and most importantly breakfast.

Write down what you eat in a diary. It is very easy to deceive yourself and think that the last time you ate chocolate cookies was one month ago when in fact it was three days before. Remember to, read the labels of the food you buy and make a conscious choice about what you eat.

Most importantly, monitor what thoughts lead to your eating. If you find yourself having high-calorie snacks, look at the way you feel just before you eat them. See what thoughts occur that lead to the emotions that happen before and during your meals. You will find that you eat to fill a void. Connecting to your Higher Self rather than eating food fills the void. Loneliness is a common fuel for feeding. A diet will not cure this. The source of your discontent is your disconnection from the part of you that is known as your Higher Self. You have the ability to correct this. ⏹

Chapter 14:

Physical Fitness and Working out

We are designed to move. Some movement is necessary for your body to continue to function optimally. If you don't use the muscles you have, they deteriorate.

Modern-day lifestyles do not call for much movement. Now that the supermarket is a short drive from you, you don't need to spend all day walking and collecting berries, and you certainly don't need to hunt for food. Exercise provides you with a way of moving that you would otherwise miss out on. Exercise increases your fitness, which makes for a better quality life.

Fitness is your ability to cope with day-to-day activity and to have something in reserve so that you can enjoy your life.

There are three components to fitness, and each needs to be optimized:

Flexibility | Flexibility helps you with your posture. Correct posture can make you feel great and give you more energy. It also helps with your range of movement, which in turn allows you to do more. Many of the things we take for granted require flexibility, like the ability to tie your shoelaces, get in and out of cars and hang up the washing. It also allows you to remain active, like kicking a ball with your kids and not tearing a hamstring.

Strength | Your muscular strength enables you to cope with everyday activities like lifting yourself up off the ground or opening the lid on a jar.

Cardiovascular fitness | Your cardiovascular system takes in oxygen via your lungs. Your heart pumps deoxygenated blood past your lungs, and oxygen is passed into your blood stream. This oxygen is carried in your blood via your arteries to feed your muscles for movement and to feed individual cells for life. Your veins, with the help of muscle movement, carry the deoxygenated blood back to your heart. The process happens all over again.

The way to achieve fitness is through exercise. Here are five benefits of exercise:

1. Exercise delays aging. It does this by improving the supply of oxygen to your cells via your circulatory system. More than half of the age-related changes in muscles, bones and joints are caused by disuse. Exercise not only prevents age-related change to your muscles, bones and joints but can also reverse these changes.

2. Exercise gives you a greater range of movement and offers strength and stability in your joints.

3. It prevents the degeneration of muscles via an improved circulatory system, which feeds your cells.

4. It gives you improved concentration because oxygen supply is plentiful.

5. Exercise makes you feel good.

There is no need for extreme exercise, but you have to do regular exercise – this is important. To stay healthy, you need to exercise every day for thirty minutes. In contrast, an elite athlete might do five hours of exercise daily. Something as simple as a walk would satisfy this.

For cardiovascular fitness you need to do at least three, thirty-minute sessions each week – something like a jog or a brisk walk, depending on your fitness level. The trick is to get your rate of breathing up. You have reached the correct intensity when you can just still talk.

You need to consider what form of movement you do. If you are walking and only using your lower body, then you need also to use your upper body. You could use hand weights to supplement your walk. You could do push-ups. You must warm up before any exercise. Warming up increases the blood flow to the muscles. Warm-up can be as simple as walking slower for the first few minutes of your walk.

The easiest way to start is walking. **Go for a walk today.** Go for a walk every day. Of course, if you haven't exercised for some time, and you are over thirty, go and see a doctor first and get a check up.

The local gym is a great place to start, as is your local council; they usually offer all types of exercise classes. Personal trainers are of great benefit if you want to achieve more. There is an enormous amount of activity you can choose from.

Again your education is relevant. The local library has tons of information, and it's free. The local newsagent and bookstore have the same at a small cost. You are responsible. You can find out more if you want. You have the power to do something. Remember you have the opportunity for movement all the time. Take the stairs in your building and walk to the local shop. I am always amazed when I am in a shopping center; of the thousands of people, I am the only one walking up the escalators.

Chapter 15:

Lifestyle and Sleep

Your lifestyle has an impact on your health. There are certain things that you do that either adversely affect your health or that you can benefit from.

Balance is essential. Balance means achieving a balance of energy in the different parts of your life. It means, give thought to and effort and action towards all the separate areas of your life. Allow time and energy for the following:

1. Yourself.

2. Your family.

3. Social activity.

4. Work.

5. Your health.

When you don't give energy to one of these areas you become unbalanced and don't feel whole. You lead an unbalanced life when you are not aware of what you are doing and give too much energy to one area. You work too much to escape the other parts of your life that require attention. You play too much to avoid the responsibility of work. When you live in awareness, you discover exactly what you are doing and what you are trying to avoid. You can then consciously adjust your life for the better.

There are two paramount areas that people often neglect. They are sleep and time for yourself.

Time to rest: Sleep

Sleep is the time that your physical body replenishes itself. When you sleep your essence or the real, you leave your sleeping physical body, and it crosses into the astral realm. The astral realm is another dimension that you are unable to see with your physical eyes. An astral realm is a place that exists but is not a physical place, as we know physical places to be. It's the world that is inhabited by thoughts and emotions, not just yours but everyone. Here in this other world, you dream.

The astral world has both a lower realm and higher realm. The upper sphere in the astral world is of greater benefit to you. It contains thoughts and emotions that are of a higher standard or are purer than those of the lower astral realm. The astral realm includes entities that are in what you call spirit form. The lower astral realm is conducive to spirits of a small vibratory nature. It contains entities of those who are under the influence of their emotions and ego. The lower astral realm also includes wandering energies of negative emotion and thoughts. Not really a beautiful place to visit. It is preferable to visit the higher realm of the astral plane.

When you dream you are sitting in the astral world near your physical body but playing a movie from your subconscious mind. You are inside this film, and it appears to be real. When you sleep someone still has to be in charge. Like when you are awake it is either your Higher Self or your Ego that is in control. Your Ego is in charge when your dreams are erratic and make no sense, jumping from one area to the next. You are still influenced by the same negative energies and patterns of thought that affect you during your waking hours. These dream images block your view of the real astral world. It happens in the same way that when you drive your car along the road and daydream, you see the images that your mind plays and not what happens along the curb, outside of your vehicle.

Where you go in the astral world is largely determined by the amount of consciousness that is present in you. The more your Higher Self is in control, the higher your consciousness. You can also influence this by what you think before you go to sleep.

What your state of mind is like as you fall sleep also determines where in the astral world you work when you are asleep. If you are emotional, or you have thoughts of a low vibration, then you will go to the lower astral realm. If you monitor your thoughts when you are falling asleep and substitute ideas that are of a higher quality or vibration, then you will go to the higher astral realm, which does not contain the ego-infested energies of other entities.

If you spend your evening as you sleep in emotion and ego, you will wake up tired. If you spend your energy in the higher astral realm, your spirit is replenished, and you wake up full of energy. You wake up tired from the lower astral realm because your mind plays out events that you need to resolve. Your subconscious mind plays images, and you don't realize you are dreaming, and the emotion involved taxes your energy. You will wake up drained.

As you go to sleep, it is important to monitor what you are thinking. Clear your mind and resolve any emotional issues that have developed during the day before you sleep. Don't go to bed on an unresolved argument. If it is a subject that spans days or years then set the mood and clear your mind with relaxing music and chant a positive mantra as you fall asleep.

Here are four other things that help the quality of your sleep:

1. Eat a light dinner. Eat it early.

2. Have quiet time before you go to bed. Dim the lights and listen to the silence. Don't watch television and then go straight to sleep.

3. Have a shower and visualize washing off all the energy of the day. You will sleep better. Try this with wild children that come home from school; give them a shower and watch them calm down.

4. Chant something that will heighten your vibration. Try the words God, Jesus or the mantra Om. I often use the mantra mentioned in an earlier chapter: "I am the soul I am the light divine. I am love I am will I am fixed design." Alternatively, fill your heart with love and goodwill, thinking of something inspiring as you drift off to sleep.

Chapter 16:

Alone Time and Meditation

For you to listen and observe what's going on with yourself and for you to discover who you are, you need to have some time that is your own.

You need to give yourself the quality time that is for you alone. Quality time is time without other people around to speak to you. It means the time that doesn't involve the television or radio.

Quality time is a time when you are doing nothing or things you love.

Sitting down and having a cigarette or driving your car is doing something.

It may be the only time that you can relax and stop moving. Allowing you some time to listen and contemplate is paramount. It allows you to get to know you. It is the only way you can intimately converse with yourself and get in touch with your Higher Self.

Like most people, you might be scared to be alone. Here are some reasons why you might be frightened:

1. When you are alone, you can listen to the voice inside your head. The voice you hear is you, your Ego or interplay between the two. Each party may reveal things that the other doesn't want to hear. In the long run, it's beneficial for you to face yourself. The day will come sooner or later.

2. When you are alone, and all is quiet, you might be sensitive to the spirit realm via direct contact or any of the numerous ways this is possible. That's very normal, and a high percentage (some people say everyone) is sensitive to the spirit realm. It scares you. The media take a lot of the responsibility in this area for their portrayal of the spirit realm as dangerous. Remember the movie The Exorcist? The media make giant leaps to create things a little more interesting for entertainment purposes. There is nothing to fear; spirits cannot harm you physically, and you have the power to tell them to go away and leave you alone. You do this by saying "go away and leave me alone." You have to believe you have the power to do this, and you can do this in your mind. Make sure you are watching your thoughts and that you mean what you say.

The quality of the spirit forms you attract is just like the quality of the friends and acquaintances you meet. If you have a conversation with an entity, then you treat them as you would when you meet any new person. Just because they are in spirit form doesn't mean they won't tell you a lie. It depends entirely on who they are and the level of consciousness they have achieved. Remember you do not automatically increase your consciousness just because you die. You are the same but without a physical body. The point here is, there is nothing to be scared of.

3. You are afraid of the concept of being one with everything. Let me explain. You struggle with the idea of becoming one because you think that you will then be gone. You think that you will cease to exist. Many people are scared to die for this very reason. When you leave your body, you are exactly as you are now but without your physical body. You have the same personality, tastes, and dislikes. You will tell the same jokes and still like or dislike the same people. You will be able to see the physical world and to a limited extent communicate with it. When you die, you will most likely remain in the illusion that you are separate and not one with everything. As you move forward through your evolution and your consciousness increases, you will be better able to integrate this concept into your being because you will be living it. Look at it this way; when you are one, you are also everyone. So you are you, and

you are everyone else at the same time. You will not cease to be you, and you do not stop existing. You will be you, but you will also be different because you have progressed, just like a child moves into adulthood and sees the world through different eyes – yet with the same eyes.

Quiet Time and Ways to Meditate

Find somewhere quiet and alone. Make sure it's somewhere you won't be disturbed. Sit and do nothing. Be with yourself. If you find yourself involved in the day's activities in your thoughts, use the technique of awareness to sit back from your thoughts. Try to do this for at least five minutes.

Meditation is simply sitting quietly and removing thoughts from your mind. It's a technique to discover you, and it allows you to look inside. Meditation enables you to communicate with your Higher Self; it makes it more conducive to inner communication because you are relaxed.

The technique requires you to sit comfortably in a chair with your back straight. Put your hands palm-up on your thighs as a symbolic gesture to receive energy. Close your eyes and proceed with one of the following methods.

There are three simple ways to meditate.

Guided meditation.

It is where someone guides you through an individual scene and places positive imagery in your mind. This type of meditation has a goal of releasing a fear or trauma. This is the easiest way to start. There are many tapes and books available on this subject. The tapes will lead you through a set script, guiding your meditation. I can highly recommend this type of meditation, especially if you are a beginner. The set script significantly improves your ability to stay focused.

Meditating on an object or sound.

It helps you to focus and prevents you from wandering about. You might chant the word 'Om' or stare at a candle.

Using a technique to neutralize any thoughts and blank the mind.

One such technique is to think of the opposite thought that enters your mind. It nullifies the direction your mind is wandering in. You do this continually and quickly, without getting stuck on thinking about anything. It has the effect of making your mind tired and shutting it down. You can also practice what you already know from this book and stand apart from your thought process and watch your mind travel past. The trick here is to relax and watch your thoughts pass and not to follow them or get involved in any way.

One of my favorite meditations is the white light cleansing meditation. Let me describe it to you.

Assume the meditation position and relax yourself by systematically moving through each of the muscles in your body and gently telling them to relax. Remain at each muscle until you feel it relax. When you are relaxed, visualize a white light above your head. The concept is God or its equivalent, so imagine that this light is such.

See the light envelop you in a tube or bubble, and make sure it completely encloses you, underneath your feet as well. Hold this image for a while to strengthen it. Visualize each of your chakras, beginning with your base chakra all the way to your crown chakra. Use a color for each in this order. Red, followed by orange, yellow, green, sky blue, indigo and violet. Imagine the white light coming down from above and into your crown chakra. Imagine the white light filling a channel down from your crown chakra through your body along your spine and out through your base chakra and down into the earth. Imagine the concept that this energy is joining God through you and to the earth. See the white light come out through each of the chakras and fill the tube or bubble that surrounds you. Imagine that the white light is purifying you, cleansing you, healing you, and connecting you to God.

To finish, imagine each of your chakras, starting with your crown chakra this time. Put a symbol that signifies protection for you, like a religious cross, over each chakra, working your way down to the base chakra. Imagine that your feet are firmly planted on the ground. You are finished.

You can meditate whenever you like. You may prefer first thing in the morning or last thing at night. Meditate when you are not tired and don't meditate on a full stomach; you will get better results when you are a little hungry. It happens because food – in particular processed and heavy foods – lowers your vibration. No wonder they say - you are what you eat. You are trying to raise your vibration and talk to your Higher Self. Meditation greatly enhances your ability to converse with your Higher Self. It helps calm your mind, and it allows you time to know yourself. It is easy to do and essential to promote positive development in your life. Start today!

Huge Thank You and Words of Gratitude!

First and foremost, Thank You for downloading this book. At the end of the day, I'm extremely grateful for every download and every purchase. It makes me smile and motivates me. I wish that every person would put their best forward for the human race. I wish you unlimited mental strength and discipline to achieve your goals and dreams.

Together we can make the difference. Hopefully you truly enjoyed my little book on inner peace. You can only achieve inner peace when your body is healthy and strong. Mind – Body – Spirit.

If you found the information useful, I would be extremely grateful if you could write a short Amazon review. It really does make the difference, and I personally read every review and take notes. I want to improve my books, so that I can provide more value to other people. I know that my future books will give you the best experience possible.

Copyright

Author: Jeremiah T. Robinson

Publisher: Transcendence Publishing

Email: transpublishing@inbox.lv

Disclaimer

Printed in Great Britain
by Amazon

32551938R00038